Unrivered

ISBN: 978-1-951979-81-2
Library of Congress: 2025939040
Published by Sundress Publications
www.sundresspublications.com

Book Editor: Alexa White
Managing Editor: Krista Cox
Editorial Assistant: Kanika Lawton
Editorial Interns: Noor Chang and Natalie Gardner

Colophon: This book is set in Sorts Mill Goudy

Cover Image: "A Self, Unrivered" by Donna Vorreyer

Cover Design: Kristin Camille Ton

Book Design: Alexa White

Unrivered

Donna Vorreyer

Acknowledgements

I am grateful to the following journals where these poems first appeared, sometimes in different forms:

Baltimore Review - "Holding On"

Beaver Magazine - "Backyard Pastoral" and "Heaven Only Knows"

The Caryatid Review – "I-XV" (published as "Crown for Cronehood")

Colorado Review - "Dysmorphia (Winter)"

The Dialogist - "Desire at Dusk"

Elysium Review - "I Fail in Many Tenses"

Fahmidan Journal - "Finding Tongues in Trees"

Harpur Palate - "Blood Line" and "Dysmorphia (Autumn)"

Identity Theory - "Coppering"

Indianapolis Review - "Post-Menopausal Weight Gain, King James Version"

Mezzo Cammin - "Love Song for Turning 60"

Moist Poetry Journal - "Everything is Terrible, and Yet the Fields"

The Night Heron Barks - "Evening Prayers for the Fearful"

petrichor - "I Contest My Body's First Eviction Notice"

Ploughshares - "Blink"

Poet Lore - "Sometimes I Want to Go Back to my Twenties"

Poetry is Currency - "Higher Barometric Pressure Leads to More Pain, Worse Function"

Redivider - "After the Change"

Rogue Agent - "Tagmata/Stigmata"

Roi Faineant - "If You Go Into the Woods Today"

Salamander - "Fragments" and "The Sacrifice"

Sho Poetry Journal - "The Sound of Just Before"

South Dakota Review - "Lessons"

Stanchion Magazine - "Continuing Education"

Stone Circle Review - "This is the Story"

SWWIM - "Naming"

Superstition Review - "Transubstantiation"

TAB: A Journal of Poetry - "Afterglow" and "Orchard After Storm"

The West Review - "To Be Honest, Not at All Like Fine Wine"

The Westchester Review - "Faith is Believing What You Cannot"

Whale Road Review - "Fifty-Nine and Feeling" and "Skeleton Key"

White Stag - "Morning Prayers for the New World"

Table of Contents

Everything is Terrible And Yet the Fields   11

I.   12

Finding Tongues in Trees   13

Transubstantiation   14

At the Farmer's Market   16

II.   17

Annual Exams, Revised Standard Version   18

Blood Line   20

Coppering   22

III.   24

The Sound of Just Before   25

Tagmata/Stigmata   26

I Contest My Body's First Eviction Notice   27

Dysmorphia (Autumn)   28

IV.   29

To Be Honest, Not at All Like Fine Wine   30

Aubade Ending in Allegro   31

Lessons   32

The Sacrifice   34

V.   35

Naming   36

Continuing Education   37

Fragments   38

Afterglow   39

VI.   40

Sometimes I Want to Go Back to my Twenties   41

Backyard Pastoral with a Little Death   42

Post-Menopausal Weight Gain, King James Version   43

Morning Prayers for the New World   44

VII.   46

If You Go Into the Woods Today   47

Dysmorphia (Winter)   48

Skeleton Key   49

VIII.   50

Fifty-Nine and Feeling...   51

Fumbling for the Light   52

Desire at Dusk   53

IX.   54

Heaven Only Knows   55

Evening Prayers for the Fearful   56

Healing   58

X.   59

Blink   60

Transference   61

Holding On   62

XI.   63

Aria for the Apostate   64

This is the Story   66

I Fail in Many Tenses   67

XII.   68

Faith is Believing What You Cannot   69

Bone Mischief   70

Love Song for Turning Sixty   71

XIII.   72

Summoning   73

Orchard After Storm   75

Lake, Dusk   76

XIV.   77

Higher Barometric Pressure Leads to More Pain, Worse Function   78

After the Change   79

Shriveled, Sweet   80

XV.   81

The Self, Unrivered   82

Everything is Terrible & Yet the Fields

are full of seed and sprouts and leaves and rain

I wear this irksome suit of flesh & yet
the fields

are scented, sweet with dirt and singing

I watch my days fall and die like embers & yet
the fields

are tangled with grasses and asters

I smile a cruel curve, a drawn bow & yet
the fields

are recycling the soft wreckage of harvest

I hate like a god hates when it is forgotten & yet
the fields

are still in love with green

I.

Forest floors are littered with bark, a flayed
shedding of skin, the strips curled and spread
like vegetable peelings, brown and decayed,
ripe for hungry ground to reclaim. Ahead
the path holds more of the same. Mountains
capped white for winter, snow settled atop
a scarf of clouds until the melt begins,
washes down the soil and erodes the rock.
Stars descend in the dust, my own shine barred
and fading as I cover my head, try
to salvage a bit of what I've lost. Scarred
by what time has stripped from memory,
I peel back the years, rub a stone smooth
with worry. I have nothing left to prove.

Finding Tongues in Trees

The bark of most trees yields to growth by splitting
or filling from within, but not so the sycamore.

Its bark flakes in uneven pieces, leaves its surface
mottled green and gray. Some mistake this for

disease, mark the trunks with Xs, call the surgeons
like we did for my father when he began to shed

and shiver, his trunk covered with sores, bruises blooming
on his limbs, the skin unable to stretch and accommodate

what roiled beneath. We did not know how to speak
to him of death, what words, until one day his frame,

wasted and bent, adorned with damage, pulsed with light,
and his heart, that most secret crocus, broke open

and poured its bright into the winter air and even when
he breathed his last, my God, there was music in that sigh,

it was joyful, and the trees all waved their arms
and taught us how to split and heal and sing.

Transubstantiation

How I wanted to be a changed thing, my body
refusing to obey. This blessed body, not as in
consecrated, but as in irritated, as in there was
not a blessed thing I could do to make a child.

Stripped of its purpose, the body shifts, becomes
a husk for shame or pleasure, sometimes both
at the same time. Becomes a temple without
an altar, an empty arc of cold midnight sky.

*

This is my body, given for you.

*

How every blessed thing becomes othered—

> a feather blessed with ink becomes pen
> a canvas with pigment becomes a world

> bread becomes a body, wine becomes blood
> bodies inked and oiled to tell their stories

> how one thing can always be another
> how even a barren woman can be a mother

*

This is my blood, shed for you.

*

How the body changes in its decline. The cheeks sink to outline the skull, the eyes wide and wild. Robust muscles fade to frail. How the child can cradle the mother now, rock her in arms she bore. How the child can cradle the father now, soothe him with hands he kissed and held. How the priest blesses their foreheads while they still can speak. How morphine is placed on the tongue. The chalice a sponge of water pressed to unmoving lips.

*

The body on earth, a temple in ruins.
It should not need to be forgiven.

At the Farmer's Market

Not my lilacs. Not my mother.
The sick-sweet overwhelms me. The flowers

are meant to entice, brimming violet-white,
and at a booth, a woman holds out a branch,

this white-haired woman working
at something beautiful and harmless.

I'd rather orange lilies with yellow tongues,
a different tent with frilly zinnias.

I'd rather avoid the memories of her,
my bedroom window, rather yearn for

those fragrant branches of memory,
their bowed purple heads. I want

home, my mother filling glass jars
with their heady scent, the same scent

I drink in now, same scent I drown in,
my arms bursting into bloom.

II.

If I worry, I have nothing. I want to prove
that age doesn't need to imply frailty,
so I set a course for unknown waters, dive
into the waves. I head deep, my feet leaving
the bottom. My arms circle, slapping
the wild foam. I find a rhythm, breathe salt
until it becomes oxygen. Fish sing
hymns, whisper secret praises, exalting
the effort of my limbs. But still the sea will waste
the sand it beats against, and my flesh is its new
shore. Reaching land, barnacled, I taste
my own sick, wrap myself in leaves. These too
will blister, crisp, collapse. I turn my head
to the elements with gilled and gutted dread.

Annual Exams, Revised Standard Version

I.
Place your chin in the cup. Lean your forehead against the rest.
The Lord opens the eyes of the blind.
Look directly at the green light.
The eye is the lamp of the body.
Do not be alarmed as the machine spits into the cornea.
When he had spit on his eyes, / and laid his hands upon him / he asked
What is the smallest line of letters you can read?
Is this one clearer? Or this one?
If your eye is sound, your whole body will be full of light.

II.
Disrobe and put on a pink gown, tied in the front,
two breasts are like two fawns, twins of a gazelle.
Wait with other women, sometimes men—
even the jackals give the breast.
When you are called, assist with stickers pressed
over moles and skin tags. Surrender your breasts
to the technician's hands.
(I was a wall, and my breasts were like towers.)
She will knead and lift them before forcing
the flesh between plates of the machine.
You are stately as a palm tree / and your breasts are like its clusters.
Feel the force and ache. Hold your breath for x-rays.
Do you not know that your body is a temple
of the Holy Spirit within you?
Watch the shadows on the nurse's face

each time she checks an image.
You are not your own.

III.
Lay your body on the white papered gurney.
Lift your feet and your dignity into cold metal stirrups.
My frame was not hidden from thee / when I was being made.
Glue your breath to a rhythm of calm,
intricately wrought in the depths of the earth.
Feel the slickened vise twist you wide.
A hand on the belly. A pinch of tissue for a test tube.
Every plant which my heavenly Father has not planted will be rooted up.
Quick afterbirth of tool and lube.
The Lord called me from the womb and from the body of my mother.
Pray it will not kill you like it did your mother.

Blood Line

I.
I wanted there to be a rivering, a signal.
        I wanted the clench and bother, the stain and solder of it,
                a desire to fit into that sisterhood. I wanted it—
desire: the clench and solder
rivering: the stain and signal
the wanting: a fit and a bother

II.
Each month, there was a river signalling
        clench. Clot and bother. Stain and stench. A doubling
                pain I did not want. The pain of that belonging—
doubling: the clench and signal
river: the stench and clot
the wanting: a bother of belonging

III.
I wanted to be a river, gathering stones, signals
        to shape in my current and birth smooth and new
                onto a shore. I wanted to be both river and shore—
gathering: the stone and current
shape: the new and smooth
the wanting: a signal for shore

IV.

Each month, there was a river signalling

      failure. Clot and carnage. Loss and empty. The breaking

           of biology's promise. A promise of a second heart—

failure: the clot and biology

carnage: the heart and signal

the wanting: an empty promise

V.

I was tired of the rivering, all its tributaries, signals

      of nothing. Flow and fallow. Useless current. More

           nuisance than nurture. I wanted to be landlocked—

flow: the useless and nuisance

fallow: the landlocked and nothing

the wanting: a signal of nurture

VI.

I wanted to be something else,

      the river dry, a signal of endings.

           Drought and flaking. Sweat and shiver.

                A new shore for this salvage.

                    I salvage a self, unrivered.

Coppering

after the painting "Copper Signal" by Dorothy Hood

how a space can be empty yet layered with ache

look how ochre flinches
at the intrusion of blue

look how the wet seeks the sand
and blue striates to a shining
trail through the ombre rock

here the crag is sharp but the gash is beauty

here breaking is not shame
but white froth and a sliver of oxidation

this valley sharp-edged as the *v* that names it
but lined with hints of healing
here cloudforms gather in the highest places

here the blue-black opens at the seam

to bleed light into everything
into my body that no longer bleeds

a body that could lie here in these
shadowed chasms
a body of blood-rocks and blue-veins
coursing bright a body that could die here

thick with life and howling
at the river's bright mouth

III.

The elements, with gilled and gutted dread,
have battered hard at every place I've lived—
wood, brick, or glass. Wrens tuck loose threads
from my head into their nests. I forgive
their thieving, know how disintegration
builds empires. I have fractured loves and bones
as a sacrifice to time. My indignation
will not turn the hands back. Home
is simply where I lay my pieces, shed my skin,
temporary storage for all my lost
and broken joys. Discard, discard, begin
again—a cycle of splinters, the cost
of settling. I unpack, struggle to remove
each fault my younger self would disapprove.

The Sound of Just Before
with a line from The Vaccines

The last night with my mother, I blinded like a snake in the blue,
shed the skin of daughter and switched roles, burst the bladder
of hope with the spoke of a morphine drip. Her breath was the color
of smoke, unable to breach the cancer's black. There on Elgin Avenue,
in the house where I was born, the sun set through living room
drapes with the liquid hiss of oxygen. My father finally slept, alone
after hours at her side, spilling his own spores of illness and grief.
My eyes and mouth swollen and sandpapered dry, furred with lack.
I could not have sapped the syrup of sleep if I tried. I don't know if
she could hear me, but I read to her, Anne and her escapades, stern
Marilla, big-hearted Matthew. My hands scabbed from alcohol swabs
and washing. *I would buy anything, try anything, take anything*
to have left my fear curled beneath clean sheets in the spare bedroom.
I wanted her to leave feeling a brighter me, one that burned only love.

Tagmata/Stigmata

At fifteen, I lay on my back
and pummeled the flesh of my belly,
willing it flatter, marked myself

amorphous, black and blue and secret.
Some dark thing staked a claim and
never left. Why would it? The skin

there silken, untouched by sun, pillowy
and safe. Today the weather beckons
and I lie on my back, let the sun honey

my eyelids, my fingertips. I trace circles
on my abdomen, try to summon
a new sweetness toward myself.

Instead I rub open a hole to where
the dark thing has hived, ever present,
buzzing its menace beneath my navel.

I tug down my shirt, lace my hands
across the seam to hold it closed.
I feed it what it needs.

I Contest My Body's First Eviction Notice

Your announcement tacked tingling to the damage
d nerves, the twist of the paper in the wind
ed way I take the stairs, the subtle swell
ing of the knees. You are disenchanted,
want me out. I confess I am a mess
y tenant, full of clumsy noise and poor
choices, my taste sometimes amiss. Pleas
e consider this: I will treat you better, but
ter your old skin, oil it back to slick, for
give your failings and doubts, our troubles twin
ing us together. Allow me to remind you
of our finer times. Yes, I will stumble,
but I sonnet gentle as a stamen. That must
be worth something. Don't give up on me yet.

Dysmorphia (Autumn)

I dig to the bottom of the suitcase to find
something warm, wool to welcome
the holy season of covering up. I've read
that any set of thighs can look desirable
in the right light, but somehow the light is
always wrong. Here in the woods
far from my usual disguises, the light
is sugared with stars, showered with meteors,
shimmered with ash and shotgun shells.
The cashier at the grocery says there hasn't
been a shooting for months so I can take off
my safety vest. Relieved to no longer be so
visible, I walk, shifting my shame from heel
to ball and back again. No one has shoveled
the should-haves, piles of them strewn
in shambles. All the paths I didn't take.
Once I had a student who carried a lemon
in his coat because he liked the way
it made his fingers smell. I admire that kind
of commitment, but I'd rather pocket a pine cone,
rough and unraveling its loud, spiny mouth.
I'd rather be that open, but my hours
of operation keep changing. When I reach
the shore of the river, a battered canoe
could be a steamship from this distance.
It could be my Titanic. It could be my ticket out.

IV.

A fault my younger self would disapprove—
this crepe-paper flesh, dark-spotted and dry,
unable to reflect light. How does youth
hold its glow? It seems too long ago that I
bounded through days, joints and muscles free
from rust. Now I seek the sun but blister
and itch at its touch. Dermatology
cannot cream this damage whole. Weird sisters
stare back at me from mirrors, from each store
window, each line doubled from toil. Troubles
multiply. I look inward to sample the core
of my body, bring forth only bubbles
of tears and blood, nothing at all worthwhile,
vials full of callous and misbegotten trials.

To Be Honest, Not At All Like Fine Wine

Vapor rises from the bath, a shoal
of ghost fish surrounding me, a mantle
of mist to conceal the damage.
I've been told some do this gracefully,
but who has the energy for grace?

Instead I cling to small miracles,
admire the intricate lace edges of kale
mapping an unknown coast. I search
a box of languages for one that buzzes
at the pitch of preservation.

But the odometer rolls forward
no matter how many times I stop
at yellow lights, horns behind me blaring.
I beg your pardon. I am trying
to make something last.

Aubade Ending in Allegro

Sludged and duct-taped, I shrink from
high beams. I used to hopscotch from thought
to thought, but now I am fallow-frozen, bamboozled
by blue light. I forget the combination to remove
my armor, clatter down the stairs in search of
tiny white bullets to load into the chamber
of my body. Still you patience your way through
my popsicle brain, my gaping hollows. Only you
can yank me out of nostalgia's amber, pull me from
my umami wallow into orange-bright morning.
So untime my limbs to limber and kiss me into
ambition. Achtung, baby. Speed up my RPMs
until I am nothing but spinning gibberish,
until I am even better than the real thing.

Lessons

after torrin a. greathouse

When I spot the snake, it is not moving. Its head inside the opening of a snail shell, mouth wide as if holding open a door. The snake's long, black body curls in the gravel, the snail shell propped like a misplaced fascinator. Walkers, runners, bikers all stop, mesmerized. A few offer up a theory. Perhaps the snake suffocated in the confined space of the shell. Perhaps it waited for the soft inner body of the snail to move and froze in the night air. In the end, none of us disturb the tableau at the side of the trail near the lake. Some will come back this way tomorrow, to see if it is gone, perhaps an easy meal for the hawks that circle the preserve. Days later, I still can't shake the image. A warning about greed. Or desire. What is worth waiting for. What is worth dying for.

I spot the open
shell, holding a
body like a misplaced

theory. Perhaps the
soft

tableau

A warning about desire.
What is worth dying for.

open

a door

wait for the

night In the end, none of us

will come back

The Sacrifice

The herd of goats whispers, *We're tired of the snow.* I whisper back, *I know,* scratch between their curved horns. Four of them chew hay, three jostle for feed, and one is on the milking table, udders full and bleating when a great boom sounds against the door. The youth brigade stomps forth in heavy boots, brandishing chains and curses, expressions that age knows by heart. I can no longer hide. I hold out my hands for shackles, and they march me into the trees, a crone in their midst, a villain from a fairy tale. If this were true, I could conjure some magic to escape. But stories are only stories, which the brigade doesn't know, so I am forced down into the cold river, made to gather stones as I grow numb, until I grow heavy enough to sink. The sun blinks through branches, the cries of the goats riding the thick air. I close my eyes. How light my eyelids feel, my hair, as I am swept beneath the current. The brigade ignores me. They will still ignore me when my bones return, will never acknowledge my haunting as they look in the mirror at their own aging faces. But the goats will know. They will butt their horns against the doors of their stalls. They will heel to the sound of my rattling.

V.

In all my callous and misbegotten trials,
age and its claws wound deepest—its murmurs
and coyote howls, its shin knives, its miles
of walks and therapies, ice packs, warmers,
razor blades hidden in the bending. Some say
this change can be managed by choice, whole food
and essential oils a sure remedy, but decay
cannot be halted, only camouflaged. Good
blood for bad. Scabs and sores that will not heal,
a chorus of reasons to hate mornings,
my imperfect DNA. The flesh flakes, congeals.
I am altered, becoming othered, morphing.
I shy away from crowds, toward isolation,
make myself a monster of my own creation.

Naming

Of course, someone has named it "apron" belly.
You know. The kind that women of a certain
age begin to show, a pouch of weight below
the navel that resists attempts at flattening.

Apron. As in part of the road where the slow
or damaged pull aside. As in *dinner on the table
when the man gets home.* As in domestic, tamed.
As in expected to toil and remain unstained.

As in tradition. As in *remember your place.* It could
be called *prosperous.* Could be *shield.* Could be
creator, battlefield, but it needs no label.
A body is a body. A woman already has a name.

Continuing Education

At the coffee shop, I seek some quiet
before the day intrudes. I push
my bifocals up my nose and think
about the senses—how, with age,
they secede from the union of the body.
First sight, which cants to shadow,
then scent, the rich roast in the air
reduced to tin or yeast. Even touch
decays, the knobbed thumbs flush
and tingling with nerves.

I drop my spoon and it clatters.
No one looks up. In this room full
of young people, I am invisible.
I could open a vein, decant my vintage,
sticky and sour, and not one
would look up from his screen,
from her botanical of floating cream.
I'd bleed out for hours. The whole
city of me could be aflame and no one
here would smell the smoke.

Fragments

The body, a mitten full of bees. A drawer
of angry brooches. The glass half-empty,
and I emptied it. A message in a bottle

that says *you must change your attitude.*
Oh, world, we are both so broken.

Maple pods helicopter down in autumn
air. I strip away the parchment to reveal
a smooth, green seed beneath.

I want to be peeled back like this.
How veined and fragile I am beneath my coat.

Afterglow

Last night I drove a long stretch of road with no street lamps
and little traffic, a sensation of floating in a dark tank
or curling inside a Rothko, engulfed and repelled
at the same time. This morning, I run through soft rain,
brush against a scribble of trailside branches, their seed pods
rattling *trust me, trust me, spring is coming and soon it will be
beautiful* but for now there is only the wet bite of winter
in the air, water from my shoes dripping into lines shaped
like my mother's face. I do not clean them up. I cannot lose her
again. Three years, and I look for her everywhere, find her
hiding in the fire, in the sink, in the sky backlit by stars.
But it's the rain that gets me. This is how mourning works:
the night she died, I ate a pretzel, soft and warm, summer
rain on the roof. Tonight, I shiver and still taste the salt.

VI.

I make a monster of my own creation,
stitched with sin and dug from dark backyards
where skunks bellow and scratch. Aberration
a name we share, shunned a status we guard.
Bring torches, bring pitchforks. We will not fear
your judgment, your jeers, or your fists.
I stock the cellar—feed it cheese, crackers, beer,
the basics to make it strong. I insist
that it takes my name. I feed it hate and lies,
prepare it for a world where pretty
faces serve as the only true currencies
for women. We don't need your pity
to survive. We may be branded and reviled,
but we are built to withstand this new-minted wild.

Some Days I Want to Go Back to My Twenties

A swirl of caramel on the tongue,
sweet and sticky, and supple-young
crocus petals shoving through snow
without apology. I know—
flowers repping youth is so cliché,
(same with chrysalis or new day)
but, swear to God, that's how it was,
a fire, a fledgling drunken buzz,
a motion, leaping from the nest
toward any shiny wreck. Fuck rest.
A slow burn, long-fuse dynamite,
some jeweled life unlived a right
I claimed as mine. I used the world
like oysters use their grit to pearl.

Backyard Pastoral with A Little Death

We try in vain to decode the soil's erosion, roots emerging wrangled and rutted from the lawn. Beneath the deck, a parabola of ants swarms the gravel toward some hidden corpse, the smell subtle yet cloying—a mouse, perhaps a bird, left by the neighborhood cats. Other small creatures burrow holes into their own sweet oblivions. Yes, there is decay, the thorn's quick nip then a bloom of blood, both of us birthed bent from an afternoon in dirt. Our shovel blades crack against clay, a fruitless clawing toward some softer landing. Pink geraniums lipstick the green with their continuous blooms, deadheaded then reborn. The grill smokes fat-slick and wicked as our dinner spits and whistles. Later, steaks devoured, we tend a different garden. So many flowers exploding in the dark.

Post-Menopausal Weight Gain, King James Version

Most uses of the word *weight* in this version refer
to gold or precious metals—payment or offering
or proof of power. This should make me value myself
more, but it's the opposite. I notice that only
once do the letters *d-i-e-t* appear referring to food.
Otherwise, they are only a part of *dieth*.

I don't want to die, so I track my calories, aspire to
*let not the greediness of the belly nor lust of the flesh
take hold of me.* I cook new foods that are healthy
and nutritious, but always return to ones that are not,
the chocolate *in my mouth sweet as honey.*

*A false balance is abomination to the LORD: but
a just weight is his delight.* I wonder who decides
upon a just weight. The doctor always says I could
stand to lose a few, but warns it will be difficult at
this age. My fitness watch says the energy I burn
should make me smaller, but it never seems to happen.

If *the belly of the wicked shall want,* then Lord,
I will remain wicked, running hard against
the odds, always hungry.

Morning Prayers for the New World

I. Matins

It's four AM and my dog is at the window,
his dim silhouette a new theology.
Ears alert, he seeks a thing he cannot see.

I rise from sweat-soaked sheets
to kneel beside him, greet this as belief.

I yawn at the bathroom mirror.
A trinity of lights flickers in my periphery,

some otherworldly ellipsis. To glimpse
the unknowable should be proof enough.
I grasp at signs, begin without answers.

II. Laud

The amen of the thrush's flute stitches
a thread through the early hours.

O God come to our aid

Part hymn, part alarm. My own throat
raw from disuse, a trifling exhalation.

O Lord make haste to help us

Something stirs against the glass.
Branches or rain or undeserved grace.

III. Prime

Dawn dapples the balcony,
dew on each new web.

Sleep's dowager, my muddy
imagination remains fertile.

Possibility tumbles me toward
another day's enterprise.

Suburban madonna, I birth
daydreams, unseeded salvation.

IV. Terce

The roadside ditch is clustered
with pinprick blooms, white
faerie flowers, bee umbrellas,
fringed and winsome as they sway.

Sometimes hemlock.
Sometimes Queen Anne's Lace.
Sometimes I can't tell and
sometimes I don't care.

The world can be lovely as it kills us.
It can be so lovely.

VII.

Built to withstand this new-minted wild,
landscape thick with critics and selfie sticks,
I abandon my monster, my patchwork child,
leave it to the mob's torches, use the old tricks.
Tripping through shadows to watch
the dry grass burn. Zig-zagging back and forth
to avoid search parties. No one will catch me,
my monster a fine decoy as I head north
to seek relief. I have read that the cold
slows the systems of the body, the heart
left alone to keep racing. I cross threshold
after threshold, perfecting the lost art
of giving up. Something pushes me on
and misfortune follows, a faithful minion.

If You Go Into the Woods Today

The forest preserve rumbles with the deep-throated song of frogs, holed up in fallen trees or testing the frigid indigo of the lake. The gulley is a bowl of fog, the water unmoving, no tides to bring forth its secrets. Algae drapes the surface, obscuring what lies beneath. Fish, certainly. A dead tree, maybe. Perhaps even a body.

Last fall, a missing man, car abandoned nearby, was found dead in these woods. There were no details provided in the press, but time and weather are not kind to flesh, and animals will do what animals will do. In this maze of trees and unmarked trails, deer and coyote disappear like magicians' tricks when startled from the path. Like the man's body, undiscovered for weeks.

How many times I must have walked right past it, unaware of him just beyond the treeline. There but not there. How many days no one knew I was there, too.

Dysmorphia (Winter)

Outside, the terrain glistens with the lie
of snow, the moon's neon vacancy.

A hare peeks from behind the white,
its softness startling as a mirror.

I wrestle my limbs to stillness,
soothe the pink cheek of fever.

I mark a line through each day I do not
do violence to myself with my tongue.

A practice I have yet to master.
There are so few lines. So much white.

Skeleton Key

My ribs pick-up sticks, my skull a bowl for cherry pits and pyrite, a cauldron to simmer the marrow into song. The teeth from my jawbone strung like pearls with a clasp of hammer and anvil, adorning my laddered neck. Beneath the leaded apron, with each thunk of exposure, hymns are humming. After, the machine shows me arranged in the usual way, and the doctor reads the film. Minor lapses in density. Arthritic calcifications. Small fissures and lesions. But he doesn't know the real story. I must break the language to tell it myself: *Once upon a time there was a girl whose skin was jeweled, whose sentences were filled with bones and ghosts.*

VIII.

Misfortune follows me. A faithful minion,
I lead it forward, gulping at the air,
each of us weary. Limping in unison,
we arrive back where I began, as speakers blare
all the old songs. Once I could remember each
word, car windows rolled down, the future bricked
into each street like a secret map. I reach
my family home, but only three clocks tick
in place of five. I decipher this message,
being good with metaphors—I cannot
outrun time's unraveling, its loss. I forage
for confidence, discover only rot
and doubt. I bend, I break, and I shake,
dropping breadcrumbs back from my last mistake.

Fifty-Nine and Feeling...

Everyone wants a shortcut to longevity—a procedure to drain
age from the face, to resupple the muscle. Some desire a natural
cure—turmeric and black pepper to erase arthritis, apple cider
vinegar to flatten a post-menopausal paunch. I have tried too
long to reverse the clock and the scale. Instead I should embrace
the softening—the world a blur without my glasses, the curves
of my body plush for touching. Laugh lines remind me that this face
has split silly with joy, and each ache and twinge is a signal flag
spelling out *alive*. I'm not just saying this so I can eat a cheeseburger
without guilt. Or maybe I am. Maybe I'm just tired of the hard sell
of Youth. Perhaps it's archaeologists who know the truth.
In any fine museum, the most revered specimens are the oldest,
the vessels and bones that speak through their shattering—
I was useful. I was beautiful. I am still here.

Fumbling for the Light

Three children in mittens raise their arms to
the gray sky, grasp at snowflakes that melt in their hands.

Our whole lives, it seems, we are reaching for something.

A baby's startled arms dart out to find
the boundaries of its body in space.

Teens swat at mosquitos, conduct
their muggy summer nights.

A festival crowd waves devil horns at the stage
as the band hits the chorus or the bass drop.

A priest blesses the congregation,
a sweeping that draws a cross.

A boxer trains with his own shadow,
an opponent only in his mind,

like my father in what the hospice nurse
called *end stage*, his mind already somewhere

in the ether, frail and flailing at the sky, me
so helpless and angry at God,

no place to throw my fists.

Desire at Dusk

[strange how]

neither age
nor breakage
quells desire

[all at once]

it blossoms
each petal
reaching for sun

[the need for]

skin on skin
the swift delight
of indulgence

[some outside force]

ferries bliss into
the bloodstream
an electric impulse

[to mute the sameness]

IX.

Dropping breadcrumbs, but avoiding other mistakes,
I lay the eggplant in the pan, keep the oil
from splatter with my finesse. Sauce and bake—
good therapy for gnarled hands and the turmoil
of illusion. This food. This kitchen. I weep
with the knowledge that I have complained
about this bounty—risen from a sound sleep
in a warm house and not howled a refrain
of thanks. Ungrateful knees. Reticent throat.
I see clouds, think only storm. Turbulence.
I look in mirrors and seek an overcoat
to hide the shame of this body. Each sense
strains to feel joy, makes it a labor,
yet compared to others, I live favored.

Heaven Only Knows

My roots are Russian and German, making me
eighty percent Bond villain, but I smile too often
to ever be convincing. Besides, I was raised to be
good, not to leave anyone out. It's how my mother
lived, my father insisting her gravestone be
carved with the phrase "friend to all," her
openness legend, every cashier and server and kid
on the block drawn into her welcoming circle.
If it is true that the dead watch over us, then
my mother is flinching at the way I throw the word
fuck around like confetti, though she once
scored one hundred points spelling *genitals*
in a Scrabble game. My father perches on my shoulder
whenever I make a purchase or a decision—*Do you
REALLY need that? Is that what you REALLY
want to do?*—and then offers me a shot of brandy
for my migraines, which I do not want or need.
It comforts to imagine them holding up numerical
placards like ice skating officials every time I write
a poem or pull weeds or clean the kitchen, always
a 9 or 10, their judgment colored by love and distance.
But with that distance, each day they grow a little
fainter, and it scares me. In my earliest memory,
my father prepared to scale and gut the catch
my brothers had pulled from the lake, and I plugged
my ears. I didn't want to hear the fish scream.
But I am listening now. In the night, I hear them
whisper, *When will you stop writing about grief?*

Evening Prayers for the Fearful

I. Nones

Now stretches the quiet afternoon.
Locusts praise the yard with their resurrection

and fragrant butterfly bushes attract
their eponyms, now tremulous with wings.

Surrounded on all sides by fertile green,
envious green—grass and leaves and fronds—

all free to steal away with the wind,
me with nowhere else to go.

II. Vespers

The grass burns where there is no shade,
the deck boards scorching my feet. The heat
is relentless, my skin brown but for blanched
breasts and belly. I hide the most vulnerable
places. Keep them under wraps. Say nothing.
Both dreams and the deer are dormant,
brain and breath slowed to the sweep of cool
from a briefly open door. All winter, I yearn
for sun and then it comes too strong. A death
that singes. A sudden wind gust to soothe,
kiss for a fevered brow. Clouds bruise the light.
The dank air parts by some invisible hand.

III. Compline

I whip the weeds until the shrapnel
shreds my calves to bleeding.

The pressure behind my eyes not illness,
but fear that cannot find utterance.

Some days I spiral into silence, others
I spiralize zucchini into noodles and pretend.

Illusion is necessary in isolation. The sky
fades light to dark, ombre to mark the hours.

The only visible star in Orion's belt
is the one that marks the hilt of his blade.

Healing

Whatever joys I find, I sort into labeled containers
for safekeeping. *Small Daily. Long-Loved Delights. Tear-
Inducing Epiphanies.* I capture each one before
grief destroys me. Once joy is safe, I use my sharpest
shears to shred the woes I've woven, unravel each thread
until a pile of fine filament snarls at my feet. Perhaps
this violence is unwarranted, these sorrows that were
mine alone now strewn around the living room, a trap
to capture you as well. Forgive me. I know I have put you
through hell, blotted the sun with my gloom although
each year with you has been sweet and more complete
than I could have dreamed. Once this floor is clean,
I promise to hold tight to spring, its light, its heat.
We'll open all the boxes. We'll find joy in everything.

X.

Compared to others, I have lived favored
by the fortune of these years—not unscathed,
just plagued by minor woes. I once heard
the lonely night roar of a lion, bathed
in the rumble and gut of it, once saw
the sun setting over an ancient
city as I hiked the old ways in. Such awe
should not be neglected. Sorry merchant
of sob stories, I make mountains from sand
and molehills. When I creak, I should celebrate
the music my body makes, its own bland
melody. Like a trout circling bait,
I try to choose: is joy a risk to take?
Blessed by breath, I must flex or I will break.

Blink

A blur of movement where it does not belong,
a white flower in the window's darkening eye.

A plastic bag, I think, caught in an updraft
or a bit of the dying yucca's autumn fluff,

but I discover it is a hawk, all muscled breast
and feathered intent, settling to perch in the tree

outside my window, to survey the yard then
fly again, gone as quickly as it came, the same way

joy arrives. Without warning. Sometimes
unrecognizable. Never promising to stay.

Transference

I ask the geranium, the fern, the lilies—
How do you go on?

They reply with pollen tongues—
Stop trying to plan.

But I have planted this heart season
after season, watered until it sprouted,

ripened to a blood-red drumming.
Yet always there is a withering.

It's time I stop asking, pry the ribs
to transplant it back into the chest,

watch it root and beat a new mantra—
let someone else be desolate.

I bind my wrists with vines and wait to blossom.
I shine and rain alone. My own sun, my own biome.

Holding On

When my wisdom teeth were pulled, the deep roots
lay bloody in the plastic tray. Everything roots—

tooth in the mouth, the mangrove tree bending
to sip the brackish bay with its roots.

My grandmother paid us a penny for each dandelion
we pulled, but only if we had its root.

Otherwise, they'll come back, she said. *If you want
a thing to die, you must kill it at the root.*

When my mother died, my father withered,
became untethered, her heart his taproot.

I pull and peel the beets for pickling, the red
seeping into my skin, blood of the root.

XI.

I am blessed by breath as I flex twigs, break
kindling to build a fire. I recall
my grandmother's words—in our time, we shake
off a pound of skin and eat a small
bushel of dirt. All those cells. All that earth.
What we lose and what we consume all part
of the cosmos, atoms formed before our birth
pulsing inside us. I stab and pull apart
the loose stitches in her quilt, passed down
to remind me, fiber, calico and wool,
her sweat pressed into each thread. Head bowed,
I squint to thread the needle's eye—a fool
for not honoring the past or creation—
and I try to mend again, each misstep salvation.

Aria for the Apostate

I try to believe but my attempts are half-
    hearted. Full of ragged hosannas.

I direct my prayers to an infinite orrery,
    a garden of stars I will never reach,
        though I once thought God lived there.

I once knelt on a pew's thin hassock,
    hands folded, and the stare from
        the crucifix frightened me.

But the choir music swelled inside my tiny
    chest, a fullness that weighted me to
        the world. A sweetness. Something holy.

Now lack of conviction hardens me.
    The hymns have turned to static.

Feedback riddled with dissembling praise.
    An arcana of nonsense that refuses to soothe.

I cannot quite recover the feeling I had
    back then, the solidity of knowing.

Still I seek connection, solace, some augury
    of divine touch. I visit the oldest cathedral
        I can find and in a stone apse, on a stone altar,

I kneel and place my ear to the ground.
    There is music here. I can almost hear it.

This is the Story

A fox at midnight. Vines of moonflowers creamy in the low glow of their namesake. Night-blooming morning glory. *Ipomoea alba.* But a lovely moment explained loses its magic.

*

The fleshy drupe of a cherry is not delicious on its own. So much trouble to remove the stone, the hands stained scarlet. Some things need to be sugared soft enough to swallow.

*

At the shore, messages written in the sand disappear. Write *Stay*, write *I miss you*, and the surf erases it. Move back, repeat on a drier canvas. Language need not be permanent to be true.

*

Better with faces than with names, better with words than numbers, my reward is stories and forgetting. Better with blankets than mirrors. Under the blankets, some forgetting hurts less.

*

This is the story: a woman went to the ocean. The air was thick and misty, and she swallowed it, greedy for sweetness. The hourglass continued its slow sieve to stillness, time a stone and a cherry.

*

This is the story: the woman was alone. She thought she heard the wind whisper *Stay*. Then a rustle behind her. A fox in the reeds. A little magic beneath a crescent moon.

I Fail in Many Tenses

I make a list of failures. It trails unwieldy,
a weighty Jacob Marley's chain.

I fail daily to rejoice: at the breath in my lungs,
at this long and irksome job of living,

at each bowl of hot soup with crackers,
at each pile of unraked leaves,

at each simple act of being. I walk everyday, I run,
but still I fail at getting faster, getting smaller.

"What are you running from?" a friend asks.
"Death," I answer, and once again I have failed

to articulate my desire to cherish everything,
from the dragonfly on my shoulder

to the hair my husband leaves in the sink after
he shaves—he shaves, he is alive!—

failed to kneel at the temple of birches and oaks
in the forest preserve, at the towering skyline

of the Loop in the distance, at the brine of an olive,
at the ache in my back (burning, yet alive!) and

I am still failing to explain, but God, give me more chances
to be bad at joy, and one of them will stick, I swear.

XII.

I am trying to mend each misstep. Salvation
requires apology, regret, taking steps
toward what I fear. This sublimation
sublime. This rebirth requiring forceps
of iron will. *I'm sorry,* I whisper
to God, to a quivering dog beneath
a bridge. I offer my wrists as tender
to snakes and wolves who bare their teeth
in my dreams. Through the thick trees, the trails
all look the same. Hard-packed, brown. Ominous,
patrolled by owls. I reach to read the braille
of bark, mark each fringe of fungus
to find my way home. The forest burns as I flee—
a cardinal sets fires from tree to tree.

Faith Is Believing What You Cannot
with a line from Shakespeare's Pericles

The windows in March show trailers of sun followed by a feature of sleet and hail. A liminal month, one where the clock steals the morning light. And when it snows in April, we grin and call it *sprinter*. Midwestern badge of honor, trading warmth for bravado. Such false pretty, the budding trees so inviting, but once outside the wind bites hard. The birds return— ducks float through ice still lacing the surface of the lake, and geese hiss pissy tantrums at any trespass. Robins twitter their sweet racket as I wake, and cardinals feather the backyard pines, bright trails of memory, signs from heaven, it is said, proof that departed loved ones are near. I want to believe this—I want it to be my mother winging through the yard, nesting in the dogwoods on the sunny side of the house. *See, where she comes, apparelled like the spring?* Her best red, heart on her wings, singing.

Bone Mischief

In the cathedral, the reliquary holds a splinter
of some saint's tibia, a sliver of femur, a tooth,
history in pockets of desiccated marrow.

On the X-ray, opaque patches of white bone
show arthritis, a narrowing of passages where
cartilage has eroded, pockets sewn shut.

In the roasting pan, the carcass of the turkey
picked clean, buttresses of bone arching over
apses of absent meat, pockets hollowed of plenty.

On the trail, the bones of a decomposed robin
splayed and spread, the hinged fingers of its wings
dwarfing its head, an empty pocket still beaked.

Beneath the dirt, remains of those I loved and
those I never knew, two hundred and six songs
rising from the pocket of every grave.

Love Song for Turning Sixty

using end rhymes from stanza 37 of Amy Lowell's "Pickthorn Manor"

First the sweat. Then the shaking.
Then the pills the doctors swore
would soothe. So much for taking
advice. The badge of age I wore
on my face not a prize. A man
can age without concern. This thing
called shame caused by the gaze
of a youthful world. I fling
my body around like a ruffian,
don't care who I pummel. I span
decades. Gold the cracks in this vase.

XIII.

A cardinal sets fires from tree to tree
as the last of summer seeps from my skin
and sets me to shiver. Epidermis of bees,
pulsing with fuzz and sting. Autumn begins
with blood and honey dripping from branches,
copper to sugar, my hair fading fast from red
to gray. Somewhere west of second chances,
I stop to gather berries, crush them in the dead
center of my palms as false stigmata.
I cannot even save myself, too far
afield to be anyone else's messiah.
The sky all clouds. So much for wishing on a star
when I can't see one. So much for ceremony.
For now, I'll continue. Come walk with me.

Summoning

Yesterday I woke early, the unfamiliar bed
twisting my back, the sun on the bedspread
a beacon. Still in the throes of half-sleep,
amorphous and dangerous as mercury,
I pulled on my boots and sweatered myself
for a walk. The trees tried their best
to autumn, but the drought and the hot
October had dulled them mostly brown.

I made my way toward the river as
a tune hummed inside my empty head,
something my parents used to listen to
about autumn leaves drifting by a window,
about the days growing long since a lover
went away. And then I missed them again.
Not again, I miss them always, but this old
song recalled their graceful dancing, how
they held each other, gliding wild around
the living room, and before I knew it,
it was night and the moon, that bastard,
reminded me that nothing lasts,
that you can walk away from mourning
in disaster-proof shoes, but you will still
leave tracks, no matter how hard you bang
the soles together before re-entering the world.

There is always evidence. And when the sky
casts its spell of cumulus and blue, the air sweet
and soft, you must admit that twilight will
arrive despite your wild devotion to the sun.
Remind yourself that you have options.
You can look to the darkening sky and say
night has fallen
as if it has landed on you.
Or you can look to the darkening sky and say
night has come
as if you have beckoned it.

Orchard After Storm

with lines from Edna St. Vincent Millay

Bark streaked black by last night's fury,
the trees hang heavy with yield,
leaves dripping in syncopated rhythm.

I reach for a pear, its yellow slick
and sinister, bittersweet. But I pull back
and leave it on the branch, remembering

the poet said *he who would eat of love must
eat it where it hangs.* I walk the broken wall
alone, smell the smoke of brushwood

still too damp to catch. Fallen unripe harvest
like stones beneath my feet, first casualties
of the sky's unrest, and *I see so clearly how*

my life must run—the griefs that will repeat,
the bloom and fall, the ruined remains. And now
the kiss of rain again, its mist full of ghosts.

You are not here, not by my side nor in the smoke
nor in the gloom. I reach again to pluck a pear.
Far and wide, ladders lean among the fruit.

Lake, Dusk

The lake laps against the rocks, a lullaby,
a soothing type of white noise.
A broad-winged bird circles slow, one
I can't identify and could never tame.
I am trying to release my need to name
the world, to slow the mathematical
progression of the hours. Age and its
maidens present as enemies,
turning the body against itself, but I have
learned to let each wound settle and close
in its own time. Learned to see not
stagnation but alteration. Learned it is
enough, this walking, this waking.
Enough to watch the bird soar weightless
over bright water. Even if it looks like rain.
Even if the banks flood—a new shore.

XIV.

For now, I'll continue. Come walk with me
among the pines, among the dead. So much
regret. Two stones in my shoe, two absentees,
lost and ruined pixels that blur the touch
I need to stem this sad unraveling.
Friends forget me. The heart locks, the blood clots,
and yet the MRI displays nothing
remarkable. Fortunate news for this
ragged traveler, but still not enough
to render me content. No mother's kiss
for my fevered brow. I roll down my cuffs
against the chill, know I am a faithless
fool. I lift my face, let go and confess.

Higher Barometric Pressure Leads to More Pain, Worse Function

When it rains, it whirs, a sad hum of stand mixer and wet
ingredients, storm clouds beaten into stiff peaks.

No, it's not like that.
I've been watching too many baking shows.

When it rains, the cliffs are shrouded in mist and the birds
circle something dead below and the dead thing is me.

That's not it, either.
When it rains, a voice says *Stop being so dramatic. It's only water.*

When it rains, my bones creak chaos. Clouds whir and needle
their way over the cliffs, that voice following them down,

all of us together at the bottom in a heap,
waiting for the sun to save us.

After the Change

I splinter the green with my animal
smell. My body a sack of hand
grenades and shattered glass.
I candy this drought with my brittle
desire. My body a crossing
of cobwebs and sugared floss.
I docile each crack with foundation
and adhesive. My body crumpled
currency that buys nothing,
found in last winter's coat pocket
like a gift. I lift it gently,
as if it will disappear.

Shriveled, Sweet

With age comes a ripening—
      a more supple sugar
      than the tart snap of youth.

If I could pass this tenderness
      back in time, I would
      tell myself to forgive myself,

that the body will soften and buckle
      under thumb, that it will
      bruise, but yield the sweetest honey.

XV.

The forests are littered with bark, all flayed.
Why worry? I have nothing left to prove
to the elements. Gilled and gutted, I dread
my faults. My younger self would disapprove
of all these callous and misbegotten trials,
making me a monster of my own creation.
But I'm built to withstand this new-minted wild
as misfortune follows, a faithful minion,
dropping breadcrumbs back from my last mistake.
Compared to others, I live favored,
blessed by every breath as I flex and break
and mend again, each misstep salvation.
A cardinal sets fires from tree to tree—
for now, I'll continue. Come walk with me.

The Self, Unrivered

I tremble at the world—lavender,
crickets, alyssum, and suffering.

I close my eyes with the moon.
I drip silver. I am not afraid.

I ask, "*Ah, Beauty, is it you?*"
I am the answer.

Notes

"I-XV" creates a heroic crown of sonnets, where the fifteenth sonnet is made up of the first lines of the previous 14.

"Annual Exams, Revised Standard Version" uses lines from the Revised Standard Version, an English translation of the Bible first appearing in 1952.

"Coppering" is an ekphrastic poem inspired by Dorothy Hood's painting, *Copper Signal*.

"The Sound of Just Before" includes a line from the song "Discount De Kooning (Last One Standing)" by The Vaccines.

"Aubade Ending in Allegro" references the U2 song "Even Better Than The Real Thing" and the album title "Achtung, Baby."

"Post-Menopausal Weight Gain, King James Version" uses lines from the King James Version of the Bible referring to the words *diet, weight, belly,* and *sweet*.

"Morning Prayer for the New World" and "Evening Prayers for the Fearful" use the names for the Roman Catholic Liturgy of the Hours, the traditional prayers for different times of day.

"Desire at Dusk" is inspired by Anne Carson's translation of Sappho's fragment 78 from *If Not Winter: Fragments of Sappho*, Vintage, 2003.

"Love Song for Turning Sixty" uses end words from stanza 37 of Amy Lowell's "Pickthorn Manor" (in the public domain).

"Summoning" alludes to the song "Autumn Leaves" written by Joseph Kosman and Johnny Mercer, original French lyrics by Jacques Prévert.

"Orchard after Storm" includes lines from the Edna St. Vincent Millay poems "Never May the Fruit Be Picked," "I see so clearly now my similar years," and "Autumn Chant" (In the public domain).

The line "Ah, Beauty, is that you?" in "A Self, Unrivered " is a quote from Herman Melville's *Billy Budd, Sailor*.

Thank You

To Erin Elizabeth Smith, Alexa White, and the Sundress editorial board who took my words to heart and made this book a reality.

To my friends and trusted first readers Rachel Bunting, Kristin LaTour, Donna Huneke, and Mike Nees.

To Joan Kwon Glass for her invaluable feedback on an early version of this manuscript.

To Patricia Smith, Aimee Nezhukumatathil, Kathleen Rooney, and Taylor Byas for their kind and insightful words about this collection. You four women have inspired me for many years and continue to do so.

To my wonderful online writing community for providing support, comfort, commiseration, and advice throughout this book's long journey to publication.

To Waterfall Glen Forest Preserve in DuPage County, Illinois, which is almost a character in these poems. This is, in some ways, a pandemic book, and walking in those trees became a significant activity for me then and remains so even now.

To Lanecia Rouse, whose encouragement and gentle manner brought me back to making visual art, including this cover piece which was created in one of her studio classes.

And always, to Jeff and Dennis. Your love and support are what keep me afloat, the shores I always return to.

About the Author

Donna Vorreyer is the author of three full-length poetry collections: *To Everything There Is* (2020), *Every Love Story is an Apocalypse Story* (2016) and *A House of Many Windows* (2013), all from Sundress Publications. Donna currently lives and creates in the western suburbs of Chicago and runs the online reading series A Hundred Pitchers of Honey and is the co-editor/co-founder of the online journal *Asterales: A Journal of Arts & Letters.*

Other Sundress Titles

Death Fluorescence
Bouwsma, Julia
$20.95

Pork Fluff
Hsieh, Tiffany
$17.95

Still My Father's Son
Hikari, Nora
$17.95

The Parachutist
Hernandez Diaz, Jose
$16.00

Pure Fear, American Legend
Dzubay, Laura
$20.00

Florence
Cooley, Bess
$16.99

D A N G E R O U S B O D I E S / A N G E R O D E S
redwood, stevie
$16.00

Spoke the Dark Matter
Whittaker, Michelle
$16.00

Back to Alabama
Smith, Valerie A.
$16.00

Good Son
Liang, Kyle
$16.00

Slaughterhouse for Old Wives' Tales
Berry, Evelyn
$16.00

Grief Slut
Berry, Evelyn
$16.00

Ruin & Want
Aaraguz, José Angel
$20.00

www.ingramcontent.com/pod-product-compliance
Lightning Source LLC
Chambersburg PA
CBHW021509090426
42739CB00007B/540